Singing the Truth:
THE STORY OF MIRIAM MAKEBE

By Jade Mathieson, Louwrisa Blaauw,
and Bianca de Jong

Library For All Ltd.

Library For All is an Australian not for profit organisation with a mission to make knowledge accessible to all via an innovative digital library solution. Visit us at libraryforall.org

Singing the Truth: The Story of Miriam Makebe

This edition published 2022

Published by Library For All Ltd
Email: info@libraryforall.org
URL: libraryforall.org

Library For All gratefully acknowledges the contributions of all who made previous editions of this book possible.

Bookdash.org

Singing the Truth: The Story of Miriam Makebe
Mathieson, Jade; Blaauw, Louwrisa and de Jong, Bianca
ISBN: 978-1-922918-92-5
SKU03040

Singing the Truth:
THE STORY OF MIRIAM MAKEBE

A long time ago, in the vast city of Johannesburg, a baby girl was born. That baby was me.

My mum called me Miriam.

Miriam Makeba.

Mum was a *sangoma*, but she also worked to make other people's homes neat and clean.

It was hard for my mum to earn enough for both of us. She started selling homemade beer to bring in more money.

The laws of the land said that selling homemade beer was wrong.

The police sent my mum to jail for six long months. I was only eighteen days old and needed my mum.

So, even though I was just a baby, I went to jail too.

As a little girl, I loved to sing.
When I was older, I helped
my mum clean houses.

Singing songs as I worked made
the chores go faster and the days
seem brighter. Singing made me
happier than I can explain.

I sang in my church, and it made others happy, too. Music has the power to bring people together.

When we were singing, we felt brave and strong.

People said my voice was a gift
and my songs were special.

I sang with other musicians,
and our music was heard
all over the world.

My home was Sophiatown,
a place of culture and music.
Sophiatown, a place where
South Africans could make
music in harmony and dance
together.

But the people who ruled
the land at the time did
not like this togetherness.
Those rulers didn't want black
and white people to be friends.

I knew it was wrong to treat people differently because of their skin colour. I did not hide my beliefs, and so those people in charge wanted me out of the country.

When I was singing in America, I was told I could never return home.

People all over the world heard
my story. My songs and my story
helped many to see how there
was no fairness in South Africa
for those with black skin.

I decided to go on singing
and telling the truth about
my country, no matter what.

The world loved my music,
and I was welcomed in many
countries. I won awards and
sang for important people
all over the globe.

My life was good, but something
was missing. I could not sing in
my home country, and people
there were not free.

Then, a wonderful day dawned when Nelson Mandela became president of South Africa. New people were in charge and the unfair laws belonged to the past.

I finally went home with new people in my heart.

After that, I could sing in a free, fair country. People of different skin colours could enjoy music together.

I helped make this happen because I was brave and strong. I sang truth in all my songs.

You can use these questions to talk about this book with your family, friends and teachers.

What did you learn from this book?

Describe this book in one word. Funny? Scary? Colourful? Interesting?

How did this book make you feel when you finished reading it?

What was your favourite part of this book?

download our reader app
getlibraryforall.org

About the contributors

Library For All works with authors and illustrators from around the world to develop diverse, relevant, high quality stories for young readers. Visit libraryforall.org for the latest news on writers' workshop events, submission guidelines and other creative opportunities.

Did you enjoy this book?

We have hundreds more expertly curated original stories to choose from.

We work in partnership with authors, educators, cultural advisors, governments and NGOs to bring the joy of reading to children everywhere.

Did you know?

We create global impact in these fields by embracing the United Nations Sustainable Development Goals.

libraryforall.org

www.ingramcontent.com/pod-product-compliance
Lightning Source LLC
Chambersburg PA
CBHW040315050426
42452CB00018B/2858